In My Defence - Life ….. .

A mother's story of her journey navigating
life after the suicide of her 21-year-old son.
Read about the impact. suicide has on
those left behind and her struggle back to
acceptance.

It is gritty, it is honest and totally compelling.

Contents

Acknowledgements

This book is dedicated to my beautiful son James Burke. He died, by suicide in April 2017 aged 21.

He will never reach his potential, never marry, never be a father. So many things are gone, wiped out in that single act. But that is the nature of suicide, its cruel, horrible, and ugly. It is not just about the physical act of taking your own life it's about the legacy of what might have been and the pain of those left behind.

I need to thank some people for their enduring belief in me, for standing beside me and never giving up. They know who they are, I do not need to mention them by name. Thank you so much, you probably don't realise how much you mean to me, how you have helped me through the darkest of times, and I hope that you will always be there.

And of course, my James, who brought me such joy during the 21 years I was blessed to have him and be his mum. I hope wherever he is, he is looking down and I hope that he is smiling, and that his pain is over. Most of all I hope he would be saying 'you smashed it mum'!

In loving memory of

James Burke

8th November 1995 – 29th April 2017

John Charles Centre for Sport

Friday 19th May 2017 at 1.30pm

Service led by John Lewis

Introduction

Why did I decide to write this guide, well I guess if you are reading it, you already know the answer to that? There must be a reason you want to read it, I mean it would hardly be classed as light reading, the word suicide alone would be enough to make sure it did not make it onto any 'light reading' list.

My only son, James, took his own life in April 2017, a date that changed my life and perspective forever. On the face of it, James had the world at his feet, he was young, 21 years, he was gorgeous (I am biased), clever, he was studying LLB Law at Leeds University.

He was an accomplished rugby player. James played in the Commonwealth Wealth games in Glasgow for Jamaica as a heritage player as his grandfather was Jamaican, it was one of the proudest moments of my life watching him with my friend John.

James's suicide was not part of the plan, it was not supposed to happen, things were ticking along quite nicely after years of struggle and wham! But then no one ever plans for such a life altering event. Someone once told me that every time you try to make a plan, God laughs! I understand that better now than you could ever imagine.

The days, weeks, months and now years since James died have been a steep learning curve for me, I have had to confront things that were buried deep inside, had to examine my own insecurities and I have been so surprised and often disappointed by the behaviour of others.

Nothing can prepare you for losing someone you adore to suicide, absolutely nothing. You will never get over the enduring and deep pain, of that I am sure, but you will learn to live with it. I am also sure about something else…..

I wish I had had this book!.

This is my perspective, its raw, its gritty, and painfully honest. There are lots of 'self-help' books on the market, lots of 'experts' queuing up to churn out advice and guidance in an almost sanitised polite way that doesn't offend anyone, often sweeping

the tough stuff under the carpet.
Unfortunately, it's the 'tough stuff' that
shapes life and changes things forever.

Suicide is not like that, no one can ever truly
understand until you are in the club. Its ugly,
its lonely, it's hard, it does not discriminate
and its forever. You are entered into a club
you never wanted to join and it's a lifetime
membership. I hope that something in thIs
book helps you on your journey. Buckle up it
will be a bumpy ride.

Sharon Burke

Searching

You may initially think that this is a strange title for a chapter of a book, especially one at the beginning, but go with it, things will become clear. Searching is one of the things you will find yourself doing and it can be relentless, searching, searching, then searching again.

It comes in waves, the need to search, to look, to find something that will make some sense of this hopeless situation you find yourself in. It's like this urge that drives you on, won't let go of the hold it has on you, no matter how you try to resist it's futile!

Only a relatively small amount of people who die by suicide leave a note, depending on which statistical information you believe that can be between 5% and 30%, but every academic paper written agrees that it is not the action of the majority. I have often wondered why this is the case. People are often fixated on whether a suicide note was left, although they often are afraid to ask me, like it would in some way justify everything, if I had a note.

I must admit, I initially bought into that false rhetoric, after all it would be something to hang onto, wouldn't it, a letter would have explained everything, made it all better wouldn't it? I now know that I was wrong, and it would make no difference, but would have only created a different set of questions, a new set of doubts and a new figurative stick to beat myself with.

Even though I know all that, I realised the truth a long time ago, I still sometimes wish I had one, even a short one would have done. My son did not leave a note and I was left with so many unanswered questions, coupled with the need to find something.

 Maybe James had hidden a letter, maybe it was in some sort of code and I was simply missing the signs. He must have left me something, he wouldn't just go, would he? I was his mum! We were close, everyone said so, I mean he left me notes to ask me to buy something from the supermarket, and this was big, never seeing me again.

I don't know what I thought he would write; I mean that's hell of a letter when you think about it. 'I'm off mum, I've had enough, sorry about everything, Bye'. That wouldn't have helped at all, but in a strange way I was distraught that he didn't leave me anything, no matter how small, no matter how ridiculous.

Desperate in my need to 'find' something meaningful I began to search, sure that I would find something that would make sense, make me feel better. I looked through everything in the house, time and time again, then looked some more. I emptied every pocket he owned, hoping to find the illusive letter. I checked every drawer and cupboard, more times than I care to admit just in case I had missed something. Still no respite, still nothing.

I flicked through books, just in case there was something hidden between the pages, checked his shoes and record cases, just in case. I convinced myself he may have posted something to me and spent days desperate for the post to arrive and the inevitable disappointment when it was just the humdrum compilation of bills and junk mail.

I even ripped up carpets to check if there was something hidden underneath, maybe he had slipped a note there? Nothing! I emptied James's room in his shared house, did it alone so that I could read the letter that would obviously be there waiting for me, even though the police had searched it before me. Nothing! I looked everywhere, under the carpet, in the rubbish bag, in socks and in every single pocket I could find. Then I looked again, my mind knew that there was nothing there, but I was driven to keep looking, daft eh?

Even now, three years on, I still find myself thinking about places I may have overlooked, still think about what I may have missed, still have moments when I'm sure it's waiting for me somewhere, but where? You will search, you will look, the drive to find something, anything, will be overwhelming at times, being ready for it to hit you will hopefully help in some way, it won't stop you, of that I'm sure.

You need to accept that you will search, sure in the knowledge that your loved one will be different, I know because I have been there, flit back there occasionally, more often than I care to admit, in sadder moments. I don't think for a minute that my advice will stop you searching, I'm sure that it won't but at least it may help you to understand that it is normal, or at least the new normal that you now find yourself living.

Stop you beating yourself up because you want to do it, help you to accept things.

Your searching may not just be physically looking through, under and within rooms, drawers, pockets or anywhere else it manifests in other ways, ways that sneak up on you, when you don't even realise you are doing it.

I was sent a video of James dancing in a nightclub hours before he died. Even though he was dancing, doing the signature moves, I was struck by how sad his eyes looked. No, not sad, empty, devoid of emotion, tired even and I've watched it a million times to see if I had missed anything. Maybe this would be the time I would spot something else. I never did. Even now I occasionally watch it, searching for that elusive sign. The sign that I know does not exist and the one I am desperate to find. I guess I will always hope that I find something, anything that means James didn't just abandon me, didn't leave me with nothing.

That is the reality I must face every day, much easier to fool myself into thinking that there is something that I just haven't found yet. You will find yourself wanting to interrogate the people who spent the last hours or days with your loved one. How did they seem, what did they say, did they mention you, did they give any signs? Did they say how much they loved you? You have to work hard to stop yourself from moving into interrogation mode, strapping them down and turning on the lamp to get the answers you crave, need.

Was there a message for you? A loud resounding no! Of course, people are wary, really wary of getting into 'that' conversation with you, they can see the desperation in your eyes, no matter how calm you present, you can never be sure how much they are sugar coating things. You will ask yourself if they are withholding anything. In fact, you can end up with more unanswered questions in your desperation to find answers to the huge question that will torture you forever.

It's hard not to become suspicious, are they holding something back? Why won't they tell you? Thoughts like that run through your mind constantly, like a bad episode of Groundhog Day on repeat, only its now how I live. Isolated, lonely, incomplete, and searching. Always searching.

Because people struggle to understand, they just do not 'get it', why would they? They feel uncomfortable, do that thing where they have sideways glances at each other, as if you can't see them, it hurts, really hurts. It's the eye rolling that really gets to you, the one that says, 'she is off again', if only they knew, but I hope they never will.

Do you remember when you were at school and someone was telling a story that was obviously untrue, far-fetched; I mean unbelievably far-fetched? Do you remember nudging your mates, rolling your eyes at each other, thinking that you were being subtle? Well, that's how it sometimes is, I've often been transported back to that fourteen-year-old emotion, only now I am on the receiving end and I'm much older, much more aware, was it as hurtful back in the day for the person on the receiving end?

You will still do this, you will question and question, even years later, you will think Why, why, why, and continue to search, running a lifetime of events through your mind, looking for signs. The impossible dream, but at least you now know that you are not losing your mind. Losing your mind would be a welcome release, I have wished for the release that insanity would give me at times, no such luck. So, I carry on searching. it' is now your new normal, as it is mine.

The Blame Game

I am not sure you will even need to be told this, you have probably already started, but be prepared to blame yourself and blame yourself for everything, no half measures, and no taking it easy on yourself.

Be ready to examine microscopically every moment, you have ever spent with the person who has died. I had years, 21 to be exact, to examine and scrutinise, run every minute through my mind, blaming myself for everything I ever did 'wrong'. Was it because I did not make it to every school assembly? I couldn't though, I was working to keep us both, pay the mortgage, put food on the table.

Would it have made a difference if I had stayed at home? Was it the time I sent him to bed early, is that when it started, the idea of suicide? Could it be because I moaned about being cold and wet after standing round a rugby pitch in the rain and wind? Why did I moan, why couldn't I just keep my mouth shut, I didn't mean it really, I was always proud of him, wouldn't have missed any of the games for the world!

If I had been a better mum surely, he would still be here, if we had had more money, more holidays, anything, he would still be here, right? If only I had not missed the signs, they must have been obvious, right? How could I have been so blind?

You WILL blame yourself, constantly, despite people who mean well saying you must not, that it was not your fault. What do they know? How could they even begin to comprehend the complex array of feelings you have? You will think that it must be your fault, depending on how close you were to the person who died, in my case my son, my only child, so the onus of guilt was and is mine and always will be.

This self-blame is enduring, even though in lucid moments you know you are lying to yourself, it will not matter, like self-harm you will keep on inflicting the pain, what else would you do. How can you move past the blame, I was his mum, I was supposed to keep him safe no matter what?

It sits around my neck, this blame, like a mediaeval instrument of torture, some days it feels so heavy I can barely stand. This self-blame is part of the inevitable psychological autopsy that you will almost definitely conduct, trust me you will always find yourself guilty. Always be punished to a whole life sentence with hard labour.

You may find yourself feeling guilty for something you did or did not do, even though you might feel like this when someone you love dies in another way, bereavement by suicide is so painful the feelings of blame and guilt are magnified over and over again. No matter what you are told, it doesn't lessen the feelings you will inevitably have the feelings of guilt and failure.

In my case I was the lone parent it was part of my job description to keep my boy safe, it was my job, I failed. bereavement by suicide is like grief on steroids with the strapline that keeps playing in your mind. He chose to leave me! This is what he wanted, to leave me, I wasn't enough to keep him here with me. These feelings can be all consuming and in a cruel twist, when you have some respite from them, you end up with a new level of guilt because you are not feeling guilty for the odd moment in time! Oh, the irony.

Knowing that this tsunami of guilt and self-blame will hit you and keep battering your senses won't mean that it will not happen, it won't lessen the pain but hopefully it will stop you from further self-blame for feeling this way. There will be enough pain without adding to it, even though you still will. No one will be able to stop you doing this someone has to be to blame after all, as that makes sense, takes away the responsibility for the decision.

Sometimes, you will want to blame someone or something else, its natural, it can be too painful to admit that your loved one was suffering from a mental health problem, depression, anxiety, stress or a combination of these or other conditions and you could not make things right. There are lots of reasons and contributory factors, circumstance and opportunity that inevitably add up to the action they took. You may want to blame the partner that finished the relationship, 'it's their fault', the employer who made them redundant, the educational establishment who didn't spot the signs, if they even showed them. All normal and very much expected.

You may even want to punish the people or person you 'blame'. I resisted because I knew deep down that no one was to blame really but it was so hard. I've spoken with people who are frantically wanting to blame someone or something. People who are in denial that their loved one was in the grip of mental ill health, depression, anxiety, stress. Instead, they blame a person, a thing or an event or series of events.

I'm not judging them, but the pursuit of retribution will never make you feel better, will never bring your loved one back and when it's over you will be left with that same empty feeling, there is no escape.

I struggled not to blame someone, really struggled, it would have been so easy to explain James actions that way. The reality is, no suicide is ever because of one single event no matter how traumatic. It may be the catalyst; it may spark a series of events, but it won't change anything. Your loved one will still be gone in the worst way imaginable and any satisfaction you feel will be short lived and will be overtaken by the gnawing emptiness that now lives within your heart.

The relationship you had with the deceased will affect how deep and how long this self-blame or the blame of others will last but it will appear, and it may be enduring and can be brutal. Be ready! Do not let it consume you. I guess I am at the extreme end really, a lone parent, James was my only child so for me I face a chasm of nothingness. Hard to explain really, I guess but to try: If you imagine getting out of a lift, thinking it was going to stop at the floor with the shops and bars, to step out and it stopped in the Sahara Desert and there is no way back into the lift. No one really shares my grief, but that is just the way it is. Life in the desert with no sunglasses or sand boots!

Grief

Be prepared for everyone to 'own' your grief, for people to tell you how you should feel, what you should do and for their 'sympathy' to decline, sharply as time goes on.

Anyone who has lost someone that they love will have experienced grief, that overwhelming sadness as you realise that you will never see that person again, never speak to them, never do anything with them. Grief after suicide is different, whilst being the same, dependant on a whole range of things, your personality, your domestic situation, and your relationship to the deceased to name but a few. All this is normal, expected and a process that everyone who is bereaved works through.

Grief is as unique, as we all are. In 2001, my father died, I was close to him, I really loved my dad, and I can remember thinking at the time that nothing could ever hurt me as much ever again, I had peaked. I felt upset, sad, desolate, all the things people who are grieving feel, dad had been ill for a long time and even though his death was expected, the pain was still raw.

Then of course there is bereavement by suicide. Grief after a suicide has been described as grief with the volume turned up full, and I think that is a pretty accurate description, a bit understated if anything. Everything is intensified, everything is starker and much more enduring. Being bereaved by the suicide of someone you love is devastating and nothing can prepare you, absolutely nothing.

Suicide doesn't discriminate, it doesn't care about wealth, status or personal circumstance, it's just a tragedy pure and simple. The loss of any child is a tragedy, people have told me that more than once, trotting. out the well-worn platitude 'you are not supposed to bury your children', which is true of course, but suicide is different, so, different.

I remember reading about the hierarchy of grief, I've searched to try and find the passage again with no luck. What it tried to do was list the contributory factors of suicide that would dictate in some way how deep and enduring the 'grief you feel would be. It asked things like, your relationship to the deceased, if it was your child you have extra points, tick. If you discovered the body, again extra points, tick. Who you lived with, on hand support, again a tick as I live alone! When I read it, I thought to myself, I heard my boy's death throes, heard him thrashing about as his body frantically fought for breath. I didn't know what it was at the time, so that's probably a few extra ticks, how sad that I am at the top of the triangle for something so awful.

When I found James, it was a seemingly ordinary Sunday morning and in that moment my life was changed forever. When I saw him kneeling there it felt as if someone had reached into my chest and was squeezing my heart, a feeling that has never really gone away. The grip is never released and on bad days it tightens so much that I can barely breathe. It's like physical pain, the type you can't take a painkiller for, they just would not work.

People initially rallied around, the death of any young person prompts a huge outpouring of grief and regret. As time goes on people are almost bored with my grief, sick of hearing it, I guess. I mean life goes on, so they say, mine is suspended. No matter what I'm doing, I am inevitably drawn back again and again.so I've learned to keep it as hidden as possible, it's like my dirty little secret I guess but it hasn't diminished one iota. It is as painful, raw, and devastating as it ever was.

Suicide grief is not just mourning the death of the person you loved, its traumatic, on a new dimension. My feelings swing from a huge sense of betrayal, I had worked hard for years, done without things to make sure James did not go without anything. I had invested 21 years, since the moment I gave birth to caring for him, being fiercely loyal to him, displaying a humungous amount of patience and it amounted to nothing! He abandoned me, left me alone. I regularly thought and still think, he decided to leave me and in private moments I still shout out 'how could you do this to me'! Selfish? indulgent? Maybe.

As a mental health professional, I know all the arguments, people have felt a need to tell me often enough that James did not know what he was doing, that he can't have been in his right mind, makes me want to scream but I have perfected the art of saying something bland like,' yes, I know'. All the time resolving mentally to not mention the way I feel again, no point.

I go back to our last conversation, last meal, last anything, all futile. I guess. The unanswered questions, the sense of abandonment, the psychological and spiritual pain that never goes away, replaying constantly the 'what ifs' repeatedly on a crazy loop that has no pause button.

Because James died by suicide, I am supposed to act in a certain way, the way he dies has stigmatised his very being and mine as his mother. People presume to know how I feel and because it's now been three years, they assume I am wallowing and that I should be 'over it, 'moving on with my life' or even worse 'getting over it'. Laugh? I nearly split my sides. You will feel a gnawing loneliness that I cannot even describe, I suppose it's part of the price to pay for loving someone and I know it's for life because I can never replace him.

Grief and trauma are distinct and different but in suicide they become inexplicably intertwined, some days it's difficult to make the distinction as the feeling is so overwhelming. I do believe that grief and joy can exist at the same time, I also know that love is enduring and continues long after death, James continues to teach me things about love and life even now.

Wortman & Latack (2015) define traumatic loss as: '*A death is considered traumatic if it occurs without warning; If it is untimely: if it involves violence; if there is damage to the loved one's body, if the survivor regards the death as preventable; if the survivor believes the loved one suffered; or if the survivor regards the death or manner of death, as unfair or unjust.'*

This resonated with me, as I had thought all those things, still do. I thought it was unfair, I thought it was unjust, James looked so awful when I found him, his beautiful face was distorted in pain and trauma. Mostly I thought, no I knew, that it was preventable, and I had the additional factors associated with suicide including the self-blame, finding his body and having no choice but to continue to live in the house where he died.

I know that you will not be able to imagine it but it's like living in his death chamber. Like being forced to revisit the scene of his death, again and again, see the marks on the door, like torture on repeat. I dig in as there is nothing else, I can do.

You will become used to the sideways glances or the look of 'here we go again' when you desperately want to talk about your loved one. The notion that it's been long enough now, you should be moving on, laughable and so very hurtful in equal measure. I have often thought I must be flawed in some way because it sometimes, well often feels like I can't express how I really feel, the pain that never goes away. The odd times, and they are getting less as my control gets better, that I allow my pain to spill over, only to be met with embarrassment or to be told what I must do, being told to 'stop it' or worse changing the subject like I had not even spoken. A mistake I am making less and less often.

This special kind of grief has taught me so many things. The world continues to move on, and you will find a way of moving forward and keeping your pain and grief inside. Allowing myself to dream or aspire is like a huge betrayal because the amount of time needed for grieving is ALWAYS, plain, and simple.

You need to be prepared for your grief to be deepened by a secondary loss, you will inevitably loose friends and maybe family who distance themselves and say it's because they don't know what to say, they obviously have not read the manual. People you thought would always be there, will disappear, become magnolia, and blend in with the background. I have been told that losing James made them sad-How do they think that makes me feel! I am sorry but I simply do not have the energy to care about how they feel, I'm too busy navigating and surviving life.

I was once invited to join a social media group, they asked me to write about the worst day of my life, so I did. They deleted my post and told me that it was too upsetting for some of the people in the group, wow, just wow.

Your grief will be all consuming, public to start with and then it will become hidden to be brought out only when you are alone. I know life would have been so different if he had still been here, people would treat me differently, for a start. You will own your grief, and of course not everyone grieves in the same way. I've learned that I have to navigate the guilt that comes with surviving and living the life I had planned for us both becoming a grandma and
being a burden to him as I got older.

There used to be an advertisement on TV, Peter Kay was telling his mum to put away the vacuum as she was going to live in a home. James used to say that as soon as I was 60 that is where I was going, we used to laugh about it, but I won't be going now, I guess. I would skip into a home if he could be here to tell me it was time.
My grief makes it a struggle to have fun and to be happy, I have elements now and then. but it is a struggle, and it will be for you too. To sum up, there is no timeline for grief, no right or wrong way, despite what you may

be told as your loss is tremendous, remember (as if you could ever forget) they chose to leave you!

The knack is to just keep putting one foot in front of the other, try to keep moving forward in the best way you can. Above all remember that you feel this way because of the love you felt, and you will not 'get over it' (whatever that means) you will just navigate a new way to live, a way to survive and a way to live this imposed life.

You will find that there are many 'experts' on the subject of grief, people who will refer to the cycle of grieving and without being harsh I usually want to just shout SHUT UP!

Part of my grief, a large part if I am totally honest is for me. Selfish grief I guess you could call it. Grief for the life I have lost, grief for the things I will never have, things I will never see, things that might have been, a lifetime of dreams – gone. Does not quite fit with any grief cycle, does not quite fit any set way of feeling. It just is.

Stigma and changed relationships.

Losing someone to suicide means you have joined a special club, one that you did not apply for, one you never thought you would be in, and one you would give anything not to be a member of. It is a lifetime membership with no loyalty perks and will affect how people see and interact with you once they 'know' the truth.

So, the worst thing imaginable has just happened, your heart is smashed to smithereens and the simple things like washing and getting dressed are a supreme effort, what is the point. At least you will be able to rely upon the support of all your friends and family eh? Of course, you will, what has happened is beyond awful, everyone will be there for you. 1,2,3 back in the room.

The reality is so different, so painful so shocking, you may as well paint a red cross onto your back and ring a bell shouting unclean as you walk down the street, let me explain.

There has been much written about stigma, usually in terms of how it stops people who are generally young from speaking out, stops them from telling someone how they feel and getting help. I agree with everything I have read, well almost.

There is little written about the stigma that will continue and escalate after they die, or the stigma those who are left behind will inevitably inherit. The reality around stigma is much deeper, much more damaging and is barely mentioned anywhere and it shocked me to the core.

There is no doubt that there is a real stigma attached to suicide and to the loved ones left behind as I have found to my cost. Your loved one will always be stigmatised by the way they chose to die, they almost cease to be a person, no matter how wonderful they were. No one says remember James, that great lad, good rugby player, no, it's always, remember James, that lad who killed himself. Imagine being defined by your death.

What other time would someone be remembered that way? People are usually remembered for what they did, where they worked, who they were related to, the way they died comes much further into the conversation.

You will also be stigmatised in the same way, I will always be the woman whose son took his own life, always. I've even been introduced as Sharon, 'you remember, it was her son who killed himself!' My face was burning I was so angry. I mean I was never introduced as Sharon, the woman whose son left wet towels in the bathroom.

You will get used to the sideways glances, although I don't think I have or ever will, maybe that's the wrong terminology, I mean it will not shock you after a time. I have lost count of the times I have entered a room or joined a group to feel the awkward silence, to witness the rest of the group stumbling around for conversation, anything that does not mention James or the dreaded S -word, suicide.

I remember being in a bar with some friends of James's, we were talking about stigma and they were shocked that things were as they were. Luther Vandross came on singing 'Never Too Much' and whenever I hear that record it stops me in my tracks as it was the record James was playing immediately before he took his own life.

When I said 'this is the last record James listened to before he died,' the awkwardness and embarrassment was tangible. I simply said, 'that's the stigma right there'. It was enough and put a dampener on the rest of the evening.

People just do not want to hear what you have to say, I don't think that it is anything personal against me, but it is really painful just the same. People I have known for years and years avoid me at all costs, I'm never invited to anything anymore, I am on the difficult pile with no way of getting off it. I remember the first time someone crossed the road to avoid speaking to me, I could not believe it, I was hurt and bloody angry. Wasn't it enough that the love of my life was gone? How dare they add to my pain! There are too many incidents to list here, well not if I want to keep this book to a reasonable length.

The times I know people have seen me in a supermarket or shop and they dart off down an aisle in case they had to speak to me. I have confronted some people, at least I used to, I don't bother anymore, no point. They trot out the inevitable line 'they don't know what to say'. I am sure you will understand that I have no sympathy for them, but as a starter for ten, they could try saying hello. Radical I know.

It's like I am not me anymore, but I am, just a sadder, much sadder version of me. So disappointing. I hate it when people make thoughtless comments about hanging themselves or killing themselves, it's just not funny. They cringe when they realise, I am there, but it just gives rise for behind the hand comments, whispers when I leave the room about me, whilst they miss the point completely about how crass their comments are.

How can we ever get rid of the stigma, help people who are suffering when it's still acceptable to joke about suicide or mental ill health in such a throw away manner. As I said earlier, and there are many scholarly articles to support what I'm saying, being bereaved by suicide is totally different to how you feel after a natural death even if their death was caused by an accident. You will suffer as I have from the 'wall of silence' from people and society, the stigma attached to suicide.

Because James died by suicide people, some people, feel they have a right to share their opinions, to give me unwanted and unhelpful advice, to say that James was selfish and a coward. I can't begin to tell you the rage I feel when I have hear this, I have walked away lots of times and I am sure they have misinterpreted my reaction. They fail to realise that my walking away protected their safety and my sanity.

A time that is overwhelming, to say the least, is made worse, if that is possible, because of stigma, I have been labelled, stereo typed and blamed for James death and the choice he made. I have had someone shouting at me in the street that James was dead, that he killed himself because of me. Like I don't think that every day. As if I have never thought that, as if I haven't examined everything I have ever done, everything I have ever said to him.

To sum up, the media and several large charities talk about the stigma that prevents men (it is almost always related to men) from speaking out about their mental fitness. They seem to have forgotten to mention the people left behind, especially the parents, you will have to find a way to live with the stigma that follows you around like a bad smell. It is hard, really, hard but you will find out which people matter and who genuinely cares, who can still see the real you and who can put their feelings aside just to be there.

Like I said earlier, I am still me, just a sadder version. I like going to places where people do not know me, don't know my story. It is so refreshing to not see the pity lingering behind their eyes, to not be spoken to as if I am stupid and have lost my ability to understand words of more than one syllable because my son is dead.

I can always tell when people know. I may bump into someone I have not seen for ages and I can instantly tell that they 'know'. Their clumsiness, their reluctance to continue the conversation, their eagerness to get away from me, minimal eye contact, its laughable really. It's also cruel and cowardly, it doesn't matter how uncomfortable you feel, those feelings can never come close to mine, only I can't walk away.

I am determined to change societies view, a huge task I know as it is far more sensational, far sexier to perpetuate the myths that surround suicide. It has become public property, knowing someone who died that way is almost a badge of honour for the predictable outpouring on social media. Makes me sad and livid in equal measures. I have to exercise great restraint to move away from the keyboard so I do not post a comment which would only add to the rhetoric that I am unstable or just an angry woman, which of course I think I may be at times, but then again, who isn't.

I often hear people talk about 'triggers', and I know people are different, react to things differently, I get that. However, if you really love someone then the trigger(s) do not happen annually, they happen every day, if that's what we are calling them. Walking around the supermarket and seeing his favourite peanut butter, going into the bathroom and there is only the towel I used, no dirty rugby kit and a million other things, the list is endless. You will have your own list.

Do not be distracted, stay away from negative people, you don't need them in your life, refuse to believe the rhetoric and just cherish your loved one's memory, there can never be any stigma in that!

Most importantly, never accept other people's views about your loved one or how you should be feeling. Navigate each day in the best way you can, the people that matter will stand by your side and still be stood by your side when you need them, even if they never truly understand how you feel, why would they? I hope that they never will.

Living life on repeat.

As a lone parent I had (have) the problem of wondering how I now describe myself, how do I now define my being? He was my only child, I was a mother, a full-time role I had occupied for 21 years and I thought it was a job for life, well at least until I died. I was the parent; I was supposed to die first after all, but it didn't work out that way.

I miss James constantly, every minute of every day, he is never far from my mind, always bubbling around in my brain. It sometimes feels like I'm trapped in a cinema that keeps playing a low budget movie over and over again.

Let me explain: Every day I find myself replaying part of our life together, not just the events of that tragic weekend, the boring mundane bits. I think about the rugby matches, and there have been hundreds, think about the times stood around rugby pitches in the cold, the rain and in blazing sunshine. Could I have done anything differently? Did I miss anything? I replay how James used to run over to collect his drink from me at the end of every match before trotting off to the changing rooms, I replay every second, desperately trying to spot the exact moment when things went wrong.

I play on repeat the holidays we had together, the time I threw his trainers into the pool in Montego Bay, he wasn't happy, could that have contributed. Replay how he was bullied at middle school and those who did the bullying are still here, did that cause it, could I have done more?

Everybody has memories, everyone has periods that they like to remember, take comfort from. Maybe it is a family holiday, maybe it's all the times that your loved one made you laugh. It is different when your loved one died by suicide, so different. Your memories will always include the extra scrutiny, looking for a sign, any sign that will give you an insight about why they went. They chose to leave you, that's the bottom line, I know all the arguments about mental health, about how people who take their own lives are not in their right mind, not thinking straight but the stark truth is they chose to go, to leave, whatever the reason, to make the pain they were feeling end, and in my case, he didn't say goodbye.

That is tough. One of the scenes I play repeatedly in my head is the last time I spoke to James, the last time I saw him alive, predictable, I guess. It was the 29th of April, the day he died. I was sat on the sofa with a cup of coffee, another usual Saturday morning. I heard banging from the kitchen, it was James coming in and he had knocked over the step ladder I had been using to change a lightbulb. It made me smile, I think that is the last time I have ever experienced a totally pure smile with no spectres in the background. Anyway, he came into the room and leant against the archway, he looked tired and he was staring at me, I mean really staring, almost looking through me. Why didn't I realise what was about to happen, why didn't I wrestle him to the ground, shout, scream, anything? Truth is I didn't know, and I continually think I should have, I replay the scene over and over to check if I have missed anything.

I asked if he was alright, he said he was tired and was going to go to bed, I twittered on about what I was going to do that day, go shopping, go campaigning and other such nonsense. If only I had known it was the last time, I would ever speak to him there was so much I would have said, I would have begged him not to go, never left his side, made him see how much I loved and needed him, but I didn't, did I miss the signs?

I told him his hair looked lovely, he had fabulous hair, it was his pride and joy, I used to find his hair in the shower, in the sink and I used to moan, I would give anything to find them now, still feel disappointed when they are not there. As he went to leave the room I asked if he was sure that he was alright, he said he was only tired. How could I have been so stupid? He didn't play with the dogs, he didn't want anything to eat, all the things he usually did but I didn't notice, it was only afterwards that I realised he couldn't get away from me fast enough, he was desperate to go upstairs, now I know why. What did I miss?

After about twenty-five minutes I heard really loud banging, it sounded like James was hitting one of the doors upstairs and I thought what on earth is he doing up there, but decided I didn't really want to know, especially if he was in a bit of a mood, I didn't want to row with him. I shouted up the stairs 'I'm off love, see you later', he didn't answer and again that was pretty normal, so I went out blissfully unaware of the horror that was to unfold.

I now know that the banging was James thrashing against my bedroom door as he died, his death throes to be exact, in a way I am thankful for the fact that I didn't know as it would have been too late to save him, and I would have had another horrendous video to add to my catalogue of repeats.

You will do the same thing, repeat over and over the last time you spoke to your loved one, I don't say the last time you saw them as I found James after he had died, that's another repeat, but the last time I spoke to him is a separate memory, distinct and yours will be too.

I am accomplished at keeping my face free of any expression, carrying on whatever conversation I am having whilst I repeat a memory of James in my head triggered by something ordinary. A record, a picture, someone mentioning something, anything, whatever your memory is. Often thinking to myself, James would love this, or I wish I could tell James this, he would 'get it'. I now live in a version of Groundhog Day, everything is replayed over and over, only with me examining everything scene by scene.

You will learn not to mention your thoughts to anyone, you will become adept at keeping things to yourself, I mean who would understand or even care, only people like me. I have been told to 'move on', to let it go, laughable. Strange isn't it, I sometimes can't remember what I have gone into the kitchen for, but I can remember every minute detail of so many days, I'm not sure what that means, but that's my life and it will probably become yours.

I also constantly remember the small things that would not mean anything to anyone else. Our 'in' jokes, the things I only spoke about with James. Our political debates where we could both say that the other one was talking rubbish. I mean there is no one else I had that connection with, how could there be. Even when we had a blazing row, I still knew he was there for me and he knew I was there for him, or at least I hope he did.

Hearing a record that he loved, or a song that linked to a time when he was younger, floods my mind with memories, usually make my eyes fill with tears and always makes my heart fill with yearning, always. The thing of never eating the Easter eggs he had been bought, they used to be lined up in the kitchen until they went out of date. So predictable! My birthday now just makes me think of the last birthday we had together, the realisation that we will never have another, so birthdays are empty and spent hoping it passes as quickly as possible.

April the month James died, no need to expand. Perhaps the worst time, if there is such a thing, is Christmas, maybe it is because it just seems to last longer, or maybe it's because there is this expectation that everyone will be jolly. Who can say?

James always pretended that he didn't like Christmas, whilst insisting that I cooked plenty of pigs in blankets, I mean, loads of them. It was one of the games we played, one of our daft routines. Me spending hours wrapping presents whilst he feigned disinterest. My friend Liz and I having huge shopping sprees in the middle of the night, filling my car with loads of goodies, James saying it was ridiculous only to have his nose in the fridge whenever he went into the kitchen.

To the outside world you will be functioning, you may even have a laugh, you will go on holiday, go shopping and live a seemingly 'normal' life but you will be hitting that repeat button in your head repeatedly. You will have all your memories on shuffle play, it's a fact, you just will!

Changed Identity

I sometimes struggle to remember who I was, who Sharon used to be, quite sad when I say it out loud.

People change as they get older, the mad nights out, nightclubbing and blowing a whole week's wage on a night out morph into a more subtle way of living. It would be strange I guess if people still wanted to be out giving it large in town every weekend wouldn't it, apologies to those who still do.

Anyway, what I am trying to say is life evolves and changes as we get older, we change, our priorities change, it is inevitable and the changes are gradual, creep up on you without you realising.

When someone you adore dies by suicide the change is instant, no straying back it's as if you go to sleep and wake up a different person. Perhaps a better way of explaining it is, it's as if you have been locked in a cupboard with a window so you can see what is happening, but you have no influence over it, because the old you is small and silent, gone forever.

How close you were and the relationship you had with the person who has died will dictate how much your identity changes, I guess who you are as a person and your desire to hang on the old, which is beyond your control, will also have a bearing.

So, I am still Sharon, I still have the same skills as I had before, still like the same music, food and places so how can my identity have changed so much you might ask, it sounds self-indulgent and ridiculous doesn't it? The dictionary says, 'The definition of identity is who you are, the way you think about yourself, the way you are viewed by the world and the characteristics that define you'. You can see how your (my) identity will be affected by such a traumatic event. One of the key things that this definition proves is that the way the world views you, has a definite impact on your identity, but then I already knew that didn't need to look it up to be sure.

I cannot control how others view me, I suppose I can to a certain extent, you know, being polite, not stealing from people and so on, everyone can do that, but that's not what I mean. When I think back to Before James died, it's like I'm thinking about someone else, someone I used to know but have no real connection to anymore.

I used to be accomplished, I had worked so hard all through my life, I held a senior responsible position at work, one in a line of positions, now I am treated by most (not all) as if I have lost my capacity to think, organise and operate at anything but a basic level. I think most people who are bereaved in whatever way will be treated differently for a short time, but it won't be enduring, it won't be as deep, and people will be much more understanding.

It's different, much different when you are bereaved by suicide. Look back at the definition and you will see that an element is the way you are viewed by the world, that is a major issue, one that you will find yourself modifying your behaviour for. Like an alcoholic may drink in secret, I mostly exhibit my sadness in that way, tears that no one will see, my secret before I try and conform again to what the world expects.

The sad thing is there are so many people lost to suicide and it's almost like the people left behind have so many additional burdens to cope with as well as their sadness and grief. Now I seem to be trapped in the cycle of making myself 'small, metaphorically of course, if only it was literal, playing to the expectations, I guess. The expectation that I have no voice, that when James died, he took my identity with him.

Anyway, back to my identity. I never really thought about it before, I was just Sharon. Sharon who worked hard, Sharon who knew stuff, James said I didn't suffer fools particularly well, I guess that was true, and Sharon who hated injustice and inequality, loved crafts, cooking and entertaining. I loved fun and having a laugh, so many things really but above all, the main affirmation of my identity was that I was a mum.

Think about how you introduce people generally, |I will wager you usually say something like this is (insert name here) she works with me, she's a nurse, a cleaner, a teacher, whatever it is. You might even say she has got twins; she is a single parent or things along those lines. Always some affirmation, hardly ever just a name, it's like we are conditioned to believe that someone in not enough just by being themself. Well, they are!!!

I'm no longer a mum, people say to me, 'yes you are, you are still James mum', and I know what they mean, I think. It usually makes me feel patronised to be honest because my membership of the motherhood club died when James did, it's past tense now and will always be that way. So, who am I now, who am I allowed to be, what do people expect? I'm no longer a mum, my greatest achievement by far.

The people I worked for attacked me unashamedly, people I had stood beside for years and years. I could have fought but decided not to, so no job. One of the things they did was make me question my ability, unforgivable but you think you know people, perhaps you never really do eh? My son, my job, my friendship circle, decimated, despite people saying we are here for you, and I'm sure that they mean it whilst they are saying it, all gone, changed beyond recognition. Is it any wonder my identity has also changed?

I sometimes want to scream, 'I am still me!' I am just lost and sad, just cut me some slack. If I am annoyed, I am human after all, it's because I'm angry about James, If I'm fed up with something, could be anything, it's because I can't move on from James, as if that could ever happen.

What does 'moving on' mean? How do you do it? Is there a manual I can loan? I hate it when people say I should move on or some such derivative, makes me scream inside, such an unthinking thing to say. I don't even know what it means just a glib throwaway comment. I try and navigate each day in the best way that I can, try and avoid situations that involve confrontation, situations where previously I would never have taken a step back from, not much point is there?

I am resigned to living like a chameleon, metaphorically of course, I don't sleep in a vivarium, fitting in where I can I suppose, now that's sad, hiding my skills and often my opinions to avoid others putting me on whatever shelf they see fit. A shelf where former mothers sit, no mothers bereaved by suicide to be exact.

I work every day to discover my new identity despite all the obstacles that life and people throw at me, it's a bit like living in a real-life version of a space invader game (now there's an age related reference), waiting for the next body blow. You may not suffer as badly as I have and do, I sincerely hope not, you may have a truly supportive group of friends and an employer who wants to help, I hope so. Even if you do, you will question your identity, you will spend times questioning who you are, some people will treat you differently, they just will, they will avoid some conversations when you are around, in case it upsets you and then they will become embarrassed when you are. That is my 'new' life, I'm afraid, difficult to accept, I often think that when James took his own life, he also took mine, or at least the life I had and knew. The life I thought was mine forever. Boring, mundane, dull I suppose, but mine!

I founded a charity, The James Burke Foundation, to provide education to as many people as possible, working towards suicide prevention. It's a cause that I am passionate about, some people think it is to glorify James, but I don't need anything to do that and they are wrong. I am driven by the need to try and prevent as many people as possible feeling the way I do. I'm introduced quite often as Sharon, who founded a charity, but that's not who I am, I am so much more.

Take time to think about your identity and do not be distracted, its hard and will take determination at a time when you barely have any strength to get through the day. The realisation that my identity, the way I was viewed had changed so much crept up on me, took me by surprise, do not let the same thing happen to you!

Feelings

Where do I even start? You will experience every feeling there is in existence, often all at once, or at least several at a time, let me try and explain.

Every waking minute of every day was full of thoughts of James. His death and the way he died consumed me like a raging forest fire, still does regularly. In those rare times when I realised that I had not thought about him or circumstances for a short while, I was eaten up by guilt. Guilt that I wasn't really that sad, albeit momentarily, I shouldn't have worried. How dare I laugh surely it was not what I deserved. Let me try and break down these feelings for you.

Fear
Fear, became a familiar visitor, creeping into almost every area of my life. Initially I

was afraid of what life would be like without James, how would I be able to cope? Afraid of the milestones that would inevitably come around, the first anniversary of his death, Christmas, birthdays, both his and mine. Afraid I would not have the strength to get through those days, as society puts so much emphasis upon us during those times. I was wrong, those days were no worse than any other, I was afraid I would never truly see the sunshine again, the jury is still out on that point.

Pining

How can one small, two syllable word be so devastating. Have you ever thought about how it feels to pine for someone? Everyone who has been bereaved will all have pined for their loved one, wished they could see them again, perhaps to tell them they love them or to say goodbye. Pining after suicide is different, it is more desperate, more urgent, you need the person to come back so you can try and put things right and change the outcome. It affects your very being, I could almost feel the longing physically, taste it and it made no difference, it still doesn't make a difference, it never will. The only difference is, the pining you feel after losing someone to suicide, is exacerbated by the overwhelming feelings of guilt you carry, making the feeling turbocharged and relentless. I am sure I will pine for my son until the day I die, I have had to learn to try and manage the feeling, lock it in a box, but it often escapes to punch me squarely in the face and send me reeling.

Regret
Loads and loads of regrets, a feeling which is very different to guilt. I regret so many things I did or didn't do, all in the knowledge I can never change anything, not ever, cant have a second chance. I just carry the regret around like an invisible heavy backpack that I cannot put down no matter how tired my arms are. There are lots of 'smaller regrets, why didn't I go to every school assembly so that I would have even more memories? The truth is, I went as often as I could, but I was a single parent with a full-time responsible job, so I had to work. Knowing that doesn't reduce my feelings of regret. The regret that usually dominates my catalogue of regrets, yes, I do have one, is the regret I feel that I didn't spot what was going on with James that fateful Saturday morning. I knew he wasn't himself so why did I let him leave the room Regret that I didn't tackle him to the ground, as if I could have, to keep him close to me. Regret that I didn't follow him upstairs, if I had I could have stopped him, surely, I

could, he wouldn't have done it if I had been there after all. I will carry this deep regret forever, if you have been bereaved in this way, it's inevitable you too will have them. They will be different, personal, perhaps trivial to others, but you will have them, part of the new, different you.

Despair/Defensiveness

I spent so much time in a state of despair which was often intermingled with defensiveness, which I suppose seems to be a strange combination of feelings, let me try to explain. When James died, I felt such deep despair, tried to figure things out with no success, couldn't find an answer because there just isn't one, I know that now.

I became defensive at the way people reacted and continue to react to me which only adds to my feelings of despair. Despair that I will never be treated differently. People felt able to criticise James, how dare they, to call him selfish or a coward, made me feel so defensive and despairing at the same time. I would have done anything to defend James in life, his death made no difference.

Whilst I wanted and want to talk about my boy, you will too, I was not prepared for the fact that some people felt that they could ask intrusive questions to satisfy their curiosity with little or no regard for the fact that this was my life. You will have times when you feel as if you are on guard, ready to defend your loved one, defend your feelings and actions, that is your right. Remember, these feelings are yours, they are part of the process you find yourself going through. Never apologise for them.

I felt a diverse and complicated range of feelings, still do, that changed from moment to moment sometimes, it's taken time and considerable resolve to control and mask them. Such a sad situation.

Anger
I barely know where to start with this, not sure I have the vocabulary to describe how I feel, but here goes. Sometimes I feel so angry I could explode, but not anger in the way I knew it before James died, not directed outwardly, more of an internal simmering rage. I am sometimes so angry with James, it ebbs and flows, its not constant anger, my love for him does not quell it. I shout and rage sometimes when I'm alone, when I can drop my pretence as no one can see or hear me. 'How could you do this to me? How could you leave me? Why couldn't you speak to me? Why here?' the list goes on and on, always

unanswered, always end up with me unable to speak through my tears, my chest feeling tight with a crushing pain that threatens to suffocate.

I get angry with myself for allowing myself to feel anger towards my poor boy, he suffered enough, is that why he went, why he left me. Could it be because he could see my hidden anger? I feel anger, mingled with despair, its sometimes difficult to distinguish between the two, towards almost everything.

Angry because I will never be a grandma, I think I would have been great. Angry at the way people judge me, how they side-line me, how they treat me as if I am invisible or to be patronised, patted on the head like a Labrador, mind they are cute, I guess. I get angry at being ignored by people I thought were friends, people I have helped and supported, angry because no one stops to consider, I mean really consider my pain, my loneliness, and my knowledge that this will last forever.

Angry that everything I had worked for was taken from me in a minute, how can that be right? I remember feeling so angry and hurt, in equal measures when I was told by a group on social media that my truth was too painful for some of the member of the group. How dare they! What did they think it looks like from my side, the side I see every day? They had asked new people to the group to describe the worst day of their life, no doubt which day that was for me. Any way I did, I thought I had toned it down a bit and my post was removed within minutes, I was told it was too painful for people to read. Says it all really doesn't it, but it made me so bloody angry, then it made me cry, the people involved never knew and If they did, I doubt that they would care.

You too will feel angry of that I am sure, you cannot control it, it just is, it's part of the way I now must live.

Loneliness
Quite an obvious emotion, you might think, and I suppose it is on the face of it. It is a constant undercurrent that washes over me daily, I often feel alone, but loneliness is much different, much different. Loneliness is such a personal thing, it affects people in profoundly different ways even though it is often lumped together, as if all people experiencing loneliness feel the same, now that's just wrong. How this emotion hits you depends on the relationship that you had with the person you have lost, your circumstances now and the life you now must live.

For me, its losing that special connection, losing the one person who understood, the person I had shared all the 'in jokes' with. The person I had built my life around and the one I thought would always be there. We had been through so much together, understood each other, now it was gone.

Loneliness that creeps into every corner of my world, when people talk about going to their child's wedding, their grandchildren, it endorses this feeling even though I am happy for them. I am never jealous, I mean I don't want their life or family, I want my own, my James.

Resignation

Resignation, what a truly apt word to describe the way I now feel. I'm resigned to feeling the way I do for the rest of my life. Resigned to having to play a role to 'fit in' with the expectations of others.

Resigned to having half a life, living in the shadows a twilight life. Resigned to never seeing James again, as if I had a choice, resigned to too many things to list here, you will be too.

Resentment

A Strange emotion to write about, I admit but it is one I feel fleetingly but surprisingly often. When I see posts on social media of new babies born to people we know, or to one of James peers. They are always beautiful, how on earth could I feel resentful of them? It's not about the babies, it's about the realisation that I will never experience the joy of being a grandma, never feel that pride or love that comes with a new grandchild.

I know that there are lots of people who will never be grandparents and I am not saying that I am special or that my feelings are more important. I am just trying to be honest and the truth is not always pretty.

I am resentful sometimes about the way I have been treated but I know it's a wasted emotion and will do no good at all, but it's a feeling I often have no control of. There are several times when I feel resentful, about life and the hand I have been dealt but I don't dwell, no point, I just try to keep moving forward, helping people and trying to make a difference.

Sadness
Goes without saying really, you would expect me to be sad, its predictable isn't it, normal even. Everyone who loses someone feels sad, of course they do, they are saying goodbye to someone they loved or were close to. This is different, much different, like sadness on steroids, the feeling runs so

deep. It permeates my very being, creeps up on me when I am not expecting it and often defies any type of logic. Why do I suddenly feel so sad when I am making a cup of coffee, James did not even drink it, so it can't be that.

Why does this sadness, like no other I have ever felt leap onto my shoulder, like someone has thrown a cloak over my head and plunged me into darkness?

Why am I much sadder than when my dad died, I adored my dad, he was awesome, and he was a huge part of my life? When he died, I can remember thinking I would never feel so sad or hurt ever again, I had peaked. I was so wrong.

I think the sadness I feel is such a complicated mixture of all the feelings I have spoken about. Mostly I think it's the realisation that I will have to live with my sadness forever. I have read lots of things that say if you learn to love yourself everything, life, will be better. Well, I hope that approach works for some people and I am sure that it does but believe me it is not that simple, if only it were. Loving myself, would not change anything, I already know my worth, my capabilities, my capacity for love and kindness, even though I have questioned them often.

I often think about when I was younger and a couple of my friends called me Sad Sack, a toy from the Raggy dolls for those of you old enough to remember. I think, no, I am sure it was because of his colour and shape, but it seems so appropriate now. I used to have a picture of them above my desk for many years as it made me smile, how could I have known I would become the real-life Sad Sack.

Take time for yourself, as often as you can. If you feel like being self-indulgent, sitting eating chocolate or binge watching something on television, just do it. Pay no heed to people who tell you how you should feel or how you should behave, we are all unique and so are your feelings.

Ignoring the Rhetoric

I think this is such an important area, one that you will be bombarded with, daily, relentlessly. It often makes me feel angry, makes me feel sad and exasperated in equal measures. Sometimes the information, the rhetoric, makes me want to laugh out loud. It would often be so easy for me to turn into a keyboard warrior, but I resist, well as often as I can to be honest.

Mental health has become 'trendy' recently, suddenly everyone and his dog is an expert and feel the need to express their views and advice on social media. There is lots of talk about suicide prevention, well there is twice a year, when it is suicide prevention time again. There is even more reference about being kind to each other and how it is good to talk, and its ok not to be ok. Let me explain how I feel about these, one at a time.

Let's start with being kind. I saw a post on Facebook a while ago, it was someone saying something like, if you identify the part of you that is making you sad and be kind to yourself, forgive yourself, love yourself you will heal. Wow! Just Wow! Some of this may be true on a very superficial level, I suppose it may work if it related to worrying about my fat arms, but depression, anxiety, stress, really? I find posts like this almost offensive and I have spoken to lots of people who are suffering for whom posts of this nature present another reason for them to beat themselves up, metaphorically and sometimes literally.

They are not able to shrug their problems off so easily, so therefore it is another example of their failure! Being kind to each other should require no instruction, we should just try to be, we are human so there will be times when we get angry or lash out, all predictable, none of us are angels or superhuman and because you are suffering doesn't mean it's apparent to other people.

I'm just saying you need to develop a resilience to some of the rubbish posted on social media or leave social media alone until you feel that you can cope, if that day ever comes. I read another post and I could not resist, I commented, I do try not to, honest. Anyway, the post said. (I'm paraphrasing slightly) that there are positives in every situation, that people should look for the positive and not bring their tales of woe! Another example of the 'coaching, new life psychobabble' that doesn't even begin to scratch the surface of anyone who is suffering. I guess if your biggest drama is not getting a table at a restaurant you fancied, it fits. However, there are some situations so huge, so bad that there can never be any positives, even though it was not aimed at me particularly, I was so angry, so hurt. There are no positives from James death, None!

Ignore the rubbish people write, they don't matter, just go with your heart, plus you won't change their opinions and it's just too exhausting to try. I mentioned this earlier, but it's so important, so hurtful, I'm mentioning it again. People will tell you to move on, they will say it's what your loved one would want, like they know. They say things like, 'it's time you moved on now', or 'the problem is you have not moved on'. Words almost fail me to be honest, well polite ones, I mean, move on! What does that even mean?

I suppose it is possible to physically move on, to get a new house, to change your car, change the places you go to. That is not moving on, although the people who tell you that you must, would have you believe it was. That is just doing things differently, which you will anyway, you have no choice. I have no idea what they mean when they say it to me and I don't believe that they do either, it's just a glib throw away comment, something that they feel they need to say. It shifts the blame for my feelings onto me, like I somehow enjoy the myriad of feelings I have, if only they knew.

I have asked people what they mean, asked them to explain what they mean and have never got an answer, so my reaction is to keep my feelings to myself, to not share how I feel so that people don't think I have failed to 'move on'. Ignore it, it is a ridiculous thing to say, its hurtful and thoughtless, but you will find that you are now fair game for other people's opinions, welcome or not. If you respond it will inevitable be because, you have not moved on!

There it is again.

Memories

We all have memories, we all remember that fantastic night out, funny days from school or maybe when you achieved something special, so I do not claim to be the only person in the world to have them.

People have memories of people they have lost, how many times have you heard someone say, 'at least you have your memories', perhaps you have said it to someone yourself. I know people mean well when they say it, but it makes me want to say, yuppy doo, that's ok then.

Remembering James is somehow different, more heightened, more precious, more private, maybe because the story was cut short and it's all I have left. The added twist is that I also have the memory of how he died, of finding him, of seeing his beautiful face distorted in pain. I know others may have seen loved ones die and will always have that memory and that is so tragic, but still, it is different. No parent, I want to say mother, but I know I need to say parent should ever have the memory of their child's suicide, not ever. I have often wished that I had one of the memory erasing contraptions that they have in the 'Men In Black' film so I could get rid of the bits I don't like, just a dream.

The main difference, I guess, is the way people feel that they can comment on what memories I have, which ones I should cherish and which ones I should not ever think about. I've been told more times than I can. mention, 'just remember the good times, If only it were that simple. If only my memory had an off switch or at least a filter, good and happy to the left, unhappy to the right. If only.

The reality is a little different, much starker and full of contradiction. On the one hand I often wish that I could switch my memories off and on the other hand I am often really scared that I will forget some detail when I need to remember everything because I can never make any new memories with him. I get panicky, when I struggle to remember the actual date, we did something, or exactly what was said or what we ate, am I forgetting him, will he eventually be erased from my mind? That thought is too horrendous to contemplate, they are all I have left after all.

Memories don't just live inside our mind, photographs, music, clothes and presents can all evoke them, transport me back to happier times. Pre-suicide days, as my life is now divided in to pre- and post-suicide episodes. I spent ages sorting through every photograph I had, wishing I had taken more, why hadn't I? We didn't have mobile phones with great cameras built into them, twenty-five years ago, we had to get films developed so photographs were often for special occasions If only I had known, I would have taken hundreds more. I would have never had the camera out of my hand. James's rugby shirts are precious to me, although I can't fully explain why. I began saving them when he was small, starting with the first ever shirt he played in when he was 5 years old, it's so tiny, it's difficult to imagine him wearing it.

The last shoes, pants, and shirt he wore on his last night out before he died, folded neatly and unwashed, they will never be washed, so important to me. If I hold them up to my nose, I can still smell him. His jewellery, which he never wore, I bought him it on special birthdays, sit in their boxes, never to be worn again. I can't part with them though, ridiculous really.

His computer which has voice recordings on it, means I can listen to his voice, which is somewhat bittersweet. I'm sometimes surprised when I listen to them, shocked really at how lovely they sound, shocked by how easy it is to close my eyes and imagine he is in the room with me. I know that they are just things, but anything that makes him seem closer to me is to be welcomed, celebrated and loved.

People say to me, 'James is always with you', but he is not, he has gone. which is why all of the memories are so precious. Remember it does not matter what anyone else says, and they will. It does not matter if anyone thinks that the things you hang onto are 'stupid' or meaningless, they are yours. Keep what you want, hold onto what memories you want, take whatever time you need to remember and reflect, after all they are your memories.

I mentioned earlier that people talk about 'triggers' but only someone who has been deeply affected by suicide understands that it is not a memory that is wheeled out once a year its part of your very being. Walking around the supermarket and seeing peanut butter, when a favourite record comes on the radio, I still have not deleted the programmes he had recorded on. the Sky planner, can't quite bring myself to do so. Hang onto every single memory you have, or let them go, only you will know what is best for you to do, me, I'm hanging on for dear life!

Life after suicide

Back to the title. Thank you for reading my words, for taking the time to try and understand, at least I hope that you did. I hope that it has made you think, will make you approach someone in my position differently.

If you are in my position, if you have lost someone you love to suicide, I hope my words have made you see that the feelings you will undoubtably have are your new normal. There is currently much talk and debate about mental health, there are many 'home grown' experts who have bought an online course and now believe that they are qualified to tell you how you should feel or what mental ill health feels like.

I have studied, gained accredited qualifications, and spoke to hundreds of people about their experiences and there is no definitive, no single example of how someone feels. There are, of course, common threads but it's such a personal experience, people become alienated, or more isolated as they can't even fit in so therefore, they must be an even bigger failure.

I have seen all the flowery stuff about how any mental health condition can be 'solved' by selflove alone, wow. There is nothing wrong with self-love, but it takes some people years to reach a point of self-acceptance. People are complicated, life is complicated sometimes, and relationships can be the most complex thing of all.

Socio/economic standing can have a direct impact on mental health, big life events can cause low mood and depression. The increased use of recreational drugs and a myriad of other reasons all contribute. Social media and the constant assault on your senses of people with seemingly perfect lives can make some feel inadequate.

I have had a steep learning curve since James died, I am embarrassed about how little I previously knew, but why would I have known? Mental ill health, or mental fitness as I prefer to call it has achieved a level of sexiness, particularly on social media, where the 'its ok not to be ok' has become a mantra. I don't disagree with the ethos, talking and encouraging people (although it is almost always aimed at men) to share how they are feeling before it overwhelms them can only ever be a good thing. However, I believe there is much more to be done, so much more That's the reason, I founded The James Burke Foundation.

The Foundation is a registered charity, whose main objective is to raise awareness off mental health issues to try and reduce the number of suicides. Or should I say the number of people who are so desperate for their pain to end they can see no other option to taking their own life. Fighting against the stigma attached to mental health (fitness) is integral to this as is education. It's not enough to 'chat' for a bit and move on, there is often nowhere for people to go.

I believe that mental health is everyone's responsibility, society must grasp the nettle and stand up to be counted if we are to try and stop this heinous loss of life. Prevention, prevention, prevention. That's the key. Creating an army of people in all walks of life who are trained to offer basic interventions, support people before their journey reaches a calamitous end. That is my goal! It has been a tough journey, we are a small charity and it often feels like we are David, taking on. Goliath every single day, but it's so important I will never give up striving.

It's been a very tough few years and I know the future will inevitably be the same, but I owe it to James to try and make a difference. So, what's next? Who knows? I get up each day, sometimes slightly disappointed or daunted that I must do it all again and try to face the day. I guess it's all that any of us can ever do, isn't it, try and keep moving forward. I am not a great one for motivational quotes but there are two things I read or listen to which seem to have great personal meaning for me.

One is a speech by Vince Lombardi, who was an American coach. He gave a speech to his team before an important game. Inch by inch, is the speech, immortalised by Al Pachino in the film 'Any given Sunday'. I'm not comparing myself to an American football team, just to the message that all we have to do to move forward is go inch by inch! A little at a time to achieve success. The other is from the Ecclesiastes Chapter 3'6, 'To everything there is a season',
A time to search and a time to count as lost,
a time to keep and a time to discard,
a time to tear and a time to mend,
a time to be silent and a time to speak.

Thank you for reading this book, for listening to my dream of creating an 'army' of trained people in every community. For allowing me to share with you my reality of losing the love of my life to suicide. They are my feelings and I make no apologies for them.

It was not my intention to shock, offend or hurt anyone, so if reading this has made you feel this way, maybe the realities of life (my life) are too much for you. But unfortunately, they are the reality of so many people's lives and until we stand up and confront the whole thing head on, we will never effect change.

It is not enough to hide behind the fact that what we have to say might make some people feel uncomfortable. To be honest, I simply don't care enough about that when our actions may and have kept people alive!

Every day I get up and it is sometimes a huge effort, just knowing that I must face another day without my boy. The days differ, as everyone's do, some better than others, none of them good, just better than others. I navigate life as best as I can, often a huge effort, but I just keep putting one foot in front of the other – 'Inch by inch'. I find myself longing to see James constantly, I know that I always will. I desperately want to talk with him, to share one of the 'in jokes' we shared, even to have a row with him would be amazing, but I know it can never be.

Death now holds no fear for me as I know, or at least I hope that on that day we would be reunited. Until then I continue shaking the proverbial tree, picking my debates with care. I used to tell a colleague and friend to 'only lace up his boots for Wembley', which meant don't argue over the things that don't matter but stand up for the things that do.

We need action and we need it now. As a society we all have a responsibility to care for each other and fight against the curse that is suicide. So, lace up your boots and come and join the army!

You can contact Sharon at: sharon@thejamesburkefoundation.com

James at The Commonwealth games 2015.

The next three pages are blank for you to be able to record your feelings. You can make whatever notes you want, anything that will make you feel better. Sometimes committing your thoughts to paper can be strangely cleansing.

Printed in Great Britain
by Amazon

24548760R00046